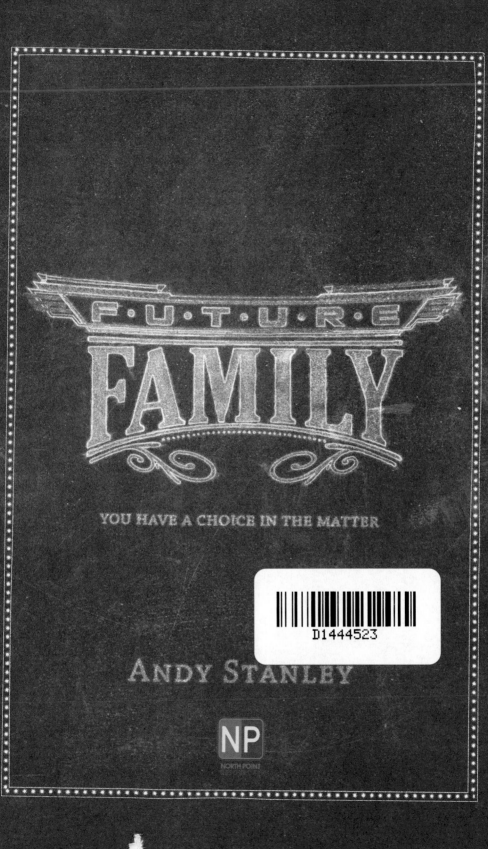

F·U·T·U·R·E
FAMILY

YOU HAVE A CHOICE IN THE MATTER

ANDY STANLEY

NP
NORTH POINT

FUTURE FAMILY Study Guide

© 2015 by North Point Ministries, Inc.

Cover design by North Point Media

Italics in Scripture quotations are the author's emphasis.

Unless otherwise indicated, Scripture quotations are from:

The Holy Bible, New International Version (NIV)

©1973, 1978, 1984, 2011 by Biblica, Inc.™

Used by permission. All rights reserved worldwide.

Printed in the United States of America

15 16 17 18 19 20 10 9 8 7 6 5 4 3 2 1

CONTENTS

Introduction by Andy Stanley 5

Session 1: Ideally Speaking 9

Session 2: Power Down 21

Session 3: Common Cause 33

Session 4: All the Fixin's 45

Session 5: Our Way, A Way 57

Session 6: The Echo 65

Leader's Guide 79

INTRODUCTION

Knowing the Past to Change the Future
by Andy Stanley

Exploring the topic of family in a small group setting is challenging because our experiences are so diverse. Some of your families are traditional and some are blended. Some of you are in first marriages and some are in second or even third marriages. Some of you are raising your biological children, some of you are fostering or raising adopted children, and some of you don't have children.

This diversity makes conversations about family complex and challenging. But at the same time, these conversations are relevant to our daily lives. So, *Future Family* zeroes in on something we all have in common: when it comes to our families of origin, none of us had a choice in the matter.

Family is difficult. The word "father" isn't emotionally neutral, is it? "Mother," "brother," "sister"—you hear those words and they stir memories, some great and some not so great.

We get to pick our friends, but we don't get to pick the families we're born into. During our teenage years, most of us wanted to pick a different family. Other people's families had different rules or didn't seem to have rules at all. They ate cereal for dinner. They slept in their clothes. Their dads were fun and their moms let them eat sugary snacks. They just seemed better than our families—at least from the outside.

Whether you loved your growing-up years or couldn't wait to move out and start fresh, you probably want your current or future family to be a step up from your family of origin. Most of us want something better for our children. To get there, you have to be intentional.

Future Family is designed to encourage conversations that help you make a connection between the family you grew up in and the family you have right now . . . or want to have in the future. We can't live intentionally as parents, spouses, children, or siblings—we can't make better decisions—if we don't understand how the past influences us.

Understanding our pasts so we can make things better for future generations is what *Future Family* is all about.

SESSION 1
Ideally Speaking

The Old Testament has example after example of family life in the ancient world. Nearly all of them are bad examples. Whether they're about Adam and Eve, Abraham and Sarah, Isaac and Rebekah, Jacob and Rachel, or King David and Bathsheba, family stories in the Old Testament are filled with deception, adultery, sibling rivalry, and general dysfunction. The first civil war in the nation of Israel was a result of a conflict between David and his son Absalom. Imagine a father-son argument that results in thousands of deaths.

If you want to know how not to approach family life, just read the Old Testament.

But something fascinating happened in the New Testament—something, well, new. In his letters to churches throughout the

Mediterranean rim, the apostle Paul applied the teachings of Jesus to family life in the first century. The result was a radical challenge to the status quo in Greek and Roman culture.

Jesus' teaching redefined the role of men, women, and children in family life. He made claims about the value of human life so bold they have reached across centuries and permeated modern American culture. We take for granted what Jesus had to say. But at the time, his teachings were a radical departure from all human culture that had existed up until that point.

By changing the value we place on individual human life, Jesus changed the way we think and function in our families.

DISCUSSION STARTER

What is one of your favorite childhood family memories?

WEEKLY READING:

Real vs. Ideal

Two thousand years ago, Jesus breathed life into culture when he said women, children, and men are all equal at the foot of the cross. The apostle Paul took the implications of that teaching and applied it to family life. In his letter to the church at Colossae, he wrote this:

Wives, submit yourselves to your husbands, as is fitting in the Lord. Husbands, love your wives and do not be harsh with them.
   Colossians 3:18–19

Why would Paul urge husbands not to be harsh with their wives? In that culture, men were harsh with their horses, their sheep, and their dogs. They were harsh with their wives, too, because wives were treated like property, not that much more valuable than the animals. It leaves a bad taste in our mouths to even think about that, but it's true. Paul's command to husbands was revolutionary.

Paul is calling men to think about women in a completely new way—as equals in the eyes of God. He's commanding them to take into account that women were culturally and politically vulnerable. They had little or no power. In his letter to the Ephesians, Paul commands husbands to "love your wives, just as Christ loved the church and gave himself up for her" (Ephesians 5:25). This means husbands are to love their wives sacrificially. It's a willing submission to her needs just as Paul calls her to submit to her husband.

This was unheard of in the first century.

Paul goes on to address the parent-child relationship:

Children, obey your parents in everything, for this pleases the Lord. Fathers, do not embitter your children, or they will become discouraged.
   Colossians 3:2–21

The surprising thing about these verses wasn't the call for

children to obey their parents. That's expected. Paul's command to fathers not to embitter their children is new. "Embitter your children" means to say something or do something that, even if it's meant to help, only discourages them. It's putting a weight on children through criticism or comparison to others. Paul knew that in his culture, fathers' tendency was to treat their children like property. He's reminding them that in the eyes of God, children are human beings, equal at the foot of the cross. A father's goal should be to gently encourage and correct his children, while respecting them as people.

This just didn't happen in Paul's day and age. Too often, it doesn't happen in our day and age either.

This brings us to the tension we'll explore throughout the rest of this study. The obedience, submission, and love Paul describes in Colossians is idealistic. There is a gap between real and ideal. People don't really behave the way Paul described, do they? You probably don't come from an ideal family. If you're married and have kids, you probably haven't created an ideal family.

What's real is that you're going through a divorce. What's real is that you're in the second marriage and it's not going so well. What's real is that you're a newlywed and it's not as easy as you thought it would be. What's real is that you've got children or you're trying to have children or your children aren't behaving or you have a prodigal child.

Paul's ideal sounds unattainable because it *is* unattainable. But here's the thing: over and over during his earthly ministry, Jesus pointed toward an ideal. He didn't condemn those who fell short, but he still talked about an ideal. In every situation, he raised the current standard.

Jesus invites us to follow him into the complexity of family life. He invites us to live in the tension between what is real and what is ideal. He urges us to embrace a standard that we have or will fall short of keeping. The alternative is to dumb down the standards so we feel better about ourselves. But that doesn't serve our families well. It doesn't serve us well because it hides the fact that we're all in desperate need of a savior.

VIDEO NOTES

_____

_____

_____

_____

_____

_____

_____

_____

_____

_____

_____

_____

_____

_____

_____

_____

_____

_____

_____

_____

DISCUSSION QUESTIONS

1. What do you hope your children experience in your family that you did not?

2. To what extent do you think children are treated like less than full people in our culture? How does that affect the way people parent?

3. How was discipline handled in your family of origin? How do you think that has or will affect your approach to discipline in your family?

4. Read Ephesians 6:1–2 and Colossians 3:18–21. How do these passages challenge your assumptions about and experiences with family life? To what extent are these passages still relevant in our culture?

5. In what family relationships do you tend to struggle with the tension between real and ideal?

6. What is one thing you can do this week in your interactions with your spouse, parents, or children to better live out the New Testament family ideal?

MOVING FORWARD

If you choose to follow Jesus' call to strive toward an ideal, you're going to feel uncomfortable about your current family situation. You're going to recognize all the ways your reality falls short of Jesus' ideal. Even though it's uncomfortable, there's something in you that refuses to lose sight of the ideal. When you think about your kids or your grandkids, you wish for them to live in the ideal . . . or as close to it as possible. You want the best for them.

Don't lose sight of the ideal even when holding the tension between real and ideal reminds you of the things you most want to forget—pain from your childhood or your failures as a spouse or parent. In his amazing mercy and grace, Jesus invites you to embrace the values that changed human civilization: *his* values.

CHANGING YOUR MIND

Trust in the Lord with all your heart
and lean not on your own understanding;
Proverbs 3:5

SESSION 2
Power Down

When it comes to family, we all feel a tension between what's real and what's ideal. Jesus acknowledged that tension, and then pushed the ideal beyond anything any of us could achieve. He raised the standard while at the same time letting us know that when we fail to live up to the standard there's forgiveness and grace. He taught an ideal but refused to condemn those who fell short. He wanted us to live with the tension and with the satisfaction that God's grace is sufficient for us when we inevitably fail.

But what does it look like to live with that tension? How does living with that tension play out in our daily lives? How can it influence and even improve our relationships with our spouses and our children?

In this session, we'll start getting practical. We'll take a look at one of the most controversial pieces of advice the apostle Paul gave to families. Nobody likes this verse in the Bible . . . especially women. But that's because it's one of the most misunderstood verses in the New Testament. It's a specific application for women of a principle Paul gave to *everyone*. People tend to miss the fact that Paul gave the principle to everyone—husbands and wives.

When put into practice, this principle can have an extraordinary effect on the quality of your family life.

DISCUSSION STARTER

Talk about a time when someone in your family went out of his or her way to help you. How did it affect your relationship with that person?

WEEKLY READING:

What Can I Do to Help?

Wives, submit yourselves to your own husbands as you do to the Lord.
Ephesians 5:22

That verse can stir a lot of negative emotions for women . . . especially when their husbands bring it up. But the first word of the verse is important: *Wives.* Paul wasn't writing to husbands. This is about how wives can apply in their marriages and families a principle taught by Jesus. It's not about husbands holding their wives to a particular standard.

In Mark 12:31–32, Jesus said that the most important commandments are to "love the Lord your God with all your heart and with all your soul and with all your mind and with all your strength.' The second is this: 'Love your neighbor as yourself.'" This kind of radical love of God and others is central to Jesus' teaching.

Later, the apostle Paul began to explore what it looks like to live out in our families the kind of love Jesus talks about. He did so in letters written to first-century Christians living all around the Mediterranean rim. His advice is direct and practical. It's simple to understand, but challenging to live out.

Ephesians 5:22 is Paul's advice to wives. But the verse that precedes it describes the general principle, applicable to every member of the family:

Submit to one another out of reverence for Christ.
Ephesians 5:21

When a family follows Jesus in their relationships with one another, here's what it looks like: everyone in the family submits to everyone else in the family. The last five words of the verse are important.

Family members don't submit to one another because they deserve it or earn it. They each submit *out of reverence for Christ.*

This principle of mutual submission is the most powerful relational dynamic. It means leveraging your time, power, and assets for the benefit of everyone else in your family. It doesn't matter whether you're the father, mother, sister, brother, cousin, aunt, or grandparent. You look for ways to get under everyone else's burdens for their sake. You do it even if they don't deserve it. You do it because Jesus got under the burden of your sin. He leveraged his power and assets for your benefit even though you didn't deserve it. He died for *your* sin so you don't have to die for your sin.

Mutual submission should be the hallmark of Christian families. If it became central in your family, it would change everything.

As we talked about last week, there will always be a divide between what is real and what is ideal. Mutual submission is ideal. You won't do it perfectly. No one but Jesus ever has.

But mutual submission is worth the effort to wrestle with that tension. Getting started is as easy as asking a question. It's a single question that mutual submission begs us to ask.:

What can I do to help?

How can I leverage who I am and what I have for your benefit? What can I do to help? Let's just practice it. That's a game changer.

If everyone in your family asked that question at least once a day to everyone else in the family, the relational dynamics in your family would change.

Asking what you can do to help is an offer of all you are for all they need. You are loaning others you. That question communicates that you're aware the other person is carrying a burden. You're aware of the responsibility you carry. Is there any way to leverage your extra time? Is there any way to leverage your talents? Is there anything you can do to shoulder some of the other person's burden so he can go further faster in whatever it is God has called him to do in relation to our home?

What can I do to help?

VIDEO NOTES

DISCUSSION QUESTIONS

1. Read Ephesians 5:21. In what ways do you try to show reverence to Christ? Do those ways extend to how you treat the members of your family? Why or why not?

2. What comes to mind when you hear the word "submit"? Why?

3. To what extent was helping one another a value in your family of origin? How has that affected the way you interact with your spouse or children?

4. What is one thing you can do to improve the way you leverage your power, influence, and resources on behalf of your spouse, your children, or your parents?

5. What is one obstacle to practicing mutual submission in your family? How can you overcome that obstacle?

6. Which member of your family do you need to ask, "What can I do to help?" What can the members of this group do to help you follow through?

MOVING FORWARD

Happiness isn't getting everyone to do what you want them to do. Happiness—especially in a family—is mutual submission. It's being willing to loan your total self to everyone else in your family.

What can I do to help?

That question forces you to lean in to your family relationships rather than pull away.

You may be wondering if mutual submission means no one is in charge. No one makes the decisions. You and your family just sit around deferring to one another. Mutual submission doesn't mean no one has authority. It's about what you do with your authority.

What would it take for you to take the first step, to be the first one in your family to ask, "What can I do to help?"

CHANGING YOUR MIND

Submit to one another out of reverence for Christ.
Ephesians 5:21

SESSION 3
Common Cause

Conflict in family is like conflict nowhere else. It's complicated and emotional. It seems to go on and on with no resolution. Part of what makes family conflict complicated is we don't process it the same way as we do conflict in other areas of our lives. We don't even process conflict the same way in terms of each member of our family. There are many different ways to process family conflict.

Some people are peacemakers. They won't even argue. Resolving conflict with peacemakers is complicated because they won't push back or argue. If you're fine, they're fine. You know they're not telling you the truth, but no matter what you do, they won't stand up for themselves.

Sulkers are down in the mouth. They don't say anything, but make it clear from their demeanor that they aren't happy with the situation.

Even when a conflict is resolved, they may claim to be fine but just mope around. Everyone knows they aren't fine.

Stuffers also claim everything is fine, but they carry the weight of a conflict around with them. Instead of saying what they think or feel, they bottle up their thoughts and emotions. Stuffers can fall victim to bitterness or holding grudges.

Then there are litigators. They're skilled and enthusiastic arguers. They always win. They're never wrong. The thing is, if you're a litigator, winning the argument works at work, on the tennis court, and with the little league umpire, but it doesn't work at home. After you've won and everybody knows you're right, it's still not over because that's how family works.

And then there are the screamers. They have to yell. They try to win arguments through sheer volume.

As long as there is family, there will be conflict. In this session, we'll explore a powerful principle introduced by James, the brother of Jesus. It's a profound relational insight that can revolutionize the way you manage conflict in your family.

DISCUSSION STARTER

What are some things you argue about with your spouse or children?

What causes these arguments?

WEEKLY READING:

Pause

The book of James was written to Christians nearly two thousand years ago. In it, James poses a question with an answer so seemingly vague that it must be rhetorical.

What causes fights and quarrels among you? Don't they come from your desires that battle within you?
James 4:1

There are many answers to that first question, right? James says there aren't. He says our conflicts come from something inside us—a desire. We want to lay blame on others. We want to say the cause of quarrels and fights in our families is something someone else has said or done. But the truth is, every conflict—especially family con-flicts—is caused by a desire that spills out on the people around us. Each of us has conflict within us that creates conflict with the people around us.-Conflict, James says, always begins with something in-side of you.

James continues:

You desire but do not have, so you kill. You covet but you cannot get what you want, so you quarrel and fight. You do not have because you do not ask God.
James 4:2

James isn't talking about murder. He's using hyperbole. But what he wrote is extraordinarily relevant to conflict in our families. Sometimes there are things you want so badly you're willing to hurt the people you care about most in order to get those things. Some of us have seen parents kill their relationships with their kids because the kids wouldn't do what the parents wanted. Some of you left home at 18 or 19 or even younger because you couldn't stand to be around your parents. But if we spoke to your parents, we'd discover they wanted you to be something or do something you didn't want to be or do. They wanted you to behave a certain way. The conflict killed the relationship.

We've all seen men destroy a woman's self-esteem. We've all seen people belittle others to the point they had no confidence in themselves. We've all seen people shame their children until they're almost afraid to be around their parents. We've all seen women with such high expectations that their words destroyed their daughters' hearts.

When you want something from someone—husband, wife, or child—you can lose perspective. In your desire to get what you want from them, you have the potential to destroy that other person. You may tell yourself you only want what's best for the other person, but the truth is you want to feel prouder, happier, more fulfilled, or better about yourself.

So, if there's basically a single source of family conflict, then what's the antidote? It's simple. When you feel conflict ramping up, you need to pause and then tell yourself six words:

I'm not getting what I want.

If in the middle of a conflict you can pause, take a deep breath, and recognize part of what you're feeling is that you're not getting what you want, that could be a game-changer. If family members would pause long enough to recognize they aren't getting what they want, it could completely change your family dynamic. You would begin to look at one another and say, "You know what? Part of the problem right now is I'm not getting what I want."

What if your husband or wife or teenage son or daughter said that? Can you imagine how the relationships in your family would change?

Let's be clear. This isn't about sweeping problems under the rug.

It's not about leaving issues unaddressed. It's about acknowledging that unmet desires are at the root of our conflicts. Acknowledging it allows us to address those desires differently.

If all family members own their part of the problem, everyone loses a little leverage and you won't fight and quarrel as much. But you have to own your part of the problem. Even if you think your part is only two percent of the problem. When you think you're in the right, you don't want to admit owning even two percent because then you have to focus on the part you own.

That's James's point. He goes on to say:

When you ask, you do not receive, because you ask with wrong motives, that you may spend what you get on your pleasures.
James 4:3

If you'll allow God to examine your heart and reveal what it is you really want that you're not getting, he will deal with it. Maybe he'll give it to you. Maybe he'll help you see that whatever it is you think will make you happy or fulfilled won't really do that at all. Either way, it'll defuse a relational bomb that may have been ready to explode in your family.

VIDEO NOTES

_____

_____

_____

_____

_____

_____

_____

_____

_____

_____

_____

_____

_____

_____

_____

_____

_____

_____

_____

DISCUSSION QUESTIONS

1. What did conflict look like in your family when you were growing up?

2. Have you ever struggled to live up to someone else's expectations? If so, what did it do to your relationship with that person?

3. When it comes to conflict, do you find it most difficult to deal with a peacemaker, sulker, stuffer, litigator, or screamer? Why?

4. How do you handle family conflict? Are you a peacemaker, sulker, stuffer, litigator, or screamer?

5. Who is suffering right now because you aren't getting your way? What do you want from him or her?

6. What can this group do to help you follow through on telling that person, *"You know what part of the problem is? I'm not getting what I want"*?

MOVING FORWARD

In an ideal family in which men and women seek to know God and follow Christ, there's a pause before the conversation. There is a come-to-Jesus, come-to-God moment in which family members pray:

"God, before I start this conversation, I want to recognize what it is I want. I want to deal with the "what I want" part before it causes a fight or quarrel. God, do in me what you need to do in me before I try to squeeze out of the people I love something that only you can give me to begin with."

CHANGING YOUR MIND

What causes fights and quarrels among you? Don't they come from your desires that battle within you? You desire but do not have, so you kill. You covet but you cannot get what you want, so you quarrel and fight. You do not have because you do not ask God. When you ask, you do not receive, because you ask with wrong motives, that you may spend what you get on your pleasures.
James 4:1–3

SESSION 4
All The Fixin's

Family is not an emotionally neutral environment. We all know this. Because family is emotional and complicated, sometimes it's tempting to tell yourself you don't care. It's a way of putting aside the pain. Your dad left when you were young. *You don't care.* Your brother is the black sheep of the family and he stole from the family. *You don't care.* You did everything you knew to raise your daughter well, but she continues to make poor choices. *You don't care.*

"I don't care" is the most harmful lie you can tell yourself about someone you're related to—especially immediate family. That's because you were created to care. If you pretend you've moved on emotionally—especially when it comes to your parents—eventually you'll be yanked back into that pain.

You may be able to avoid it in your twenties and thirties, but in your forties or fifties it'll come back to haunt you. Something will trigger a childhood emotion, and you'll realize you really *do* care. Your parents may not even be alive anymore, but it won't matter. You'll be neck deep in emotions you've spent your life refusing to acknowledge or deal with.

You were created to care. When you start whispering to yourself or telling other people around that you've just moved on from a difficult event or season, you need to pay attention because that's a dangerous lie. In this session, we're going to explore how to begin or continue the process of reconciliation with family members.

DISCUSSION STARTER

Talk about a time when someone else made the first move to end an argument without trying to force you to admit you were wrong. How did it make you feel?

WEEKLY READING

In Spite Of

For those who follow him, Jesus leaves no wiggle room when it comes to pursuing reconciliation. Even if reconciliation never happens, it's worth pursuing. Even if you can't return to the relationship because it was unhealthy or abusive, it's worth pursuing. That's because the pursuit of reconciliation is good for you . . . regardless of the results.

The apostle Paul explains the power of reconciliation in one of his letters to the church at Corinth.

For Christ's love compels us, because we are convinced that one died for all, and therefore all died. And he died for all, that those who live should no longer live for themselves but for him who died for them and was raised again.
2 Corinthians 5:14–15

Why does Christ's love compel us? Because he died on our behalf. That idea is clear. The second half of the verse—the idea that "all died"—is less clear. What Paul means is that because Jesus gave his life for us, we are to give our lives for him. Jesus said no to what was in his best interests for our best interests. In response, we should say no to ourselves for his best interests.

To "die" in this instance means that when circumstances get difficult and you have to make a decision and you know what God wants you to do, you say no to yourself and yes to God. The reason you say yes to God is that Jesus died for you. Since God was reconciled to us through Jesus, out of sheer gratitude we should say yes to him no matter what he wants us to do.

Paul continues:

All this is from God, who reconciled us to himself through Christ and gave us the ministry of reconciliation: that God was reconciling the world to himself in Christ, not counting people's sins against them. And he has committed to us the message of reconciliation.
2 Corinthians 5:18–19

No matter what people have done, they can be reconciled with God. They don't even have to clean up their acts first. He'll accept them just as they are. That's the message of Christianity. We were given that message to live out and share with the people all around us. The implications of that idea are huge in terms of what it says about how we're to think about other people.

We're not to count their sins against them. We're to forgive . . . in spite of people's failures and sin. That's hard.

Our message is that people can be reconciled to God in spite of their sin. That's what Jesus wants us to communicate to our selfish sister-in-law, deadbeat father, or brother whose reckless decisions have taken his life right off the rails.

You may have a person in your family who hurt you so profoundly you have reason to hate him or her. It would be easy to claim that the reconciliation Paul describes doesn't apply to you because your situation is so extreme. Or maybe you have a friend who has suffered unimaginably at the hands of a relative. Surely, even the apostle Paul would agree that that friend's story is the exception that proves the rule.

Reconciliation isn't about talking about past pains one more time. It's not about justifying yourself to someone else. It's not about getting someone to see the situation the way you see it. It's not about bringing up the past. It's not about finally getting the other person to admit he or she was wrong. It's not about convicting, coercing, or changing. Reconciliation is "in spite of." It's about moving forward in relationship in spite of what's happened.

"While we were still sinners, Christ died for us" (Romans 5:8b). He died for us in spite of the fact that we didn't deserve it.

VIDEO NOTES

DISCUSSION QUESTIONS

1. Talk about a time when you received affirmation from your parent or your child. How did it make you feel?

2. How has your relationship with your father made a relationship with God easier or more difficult?

3. Read 2 Corinthians 5:14–15. What would it look like for you to "no longer live for yourself" in your family?

4. Do you think it's reasonable to pursue the kind of radical reconciliation the apostle Paul describes? Why or why not?

5. About whom in your family do you say, "I don't care"? What makes your relationship with that person challenging?

6. What can you do this week to open a door, extend a hand, or lean in the direction of that person? What can this group do to support you?

MOVING FORWARD

When you reconcile with family members regardless of their behavior, some people will think you're condoning that behavior. You're not. You're doing the uncomfortable thing. You're reconciling. You're not there to accuse or condemn. You're not there to help the other person see how he or she was wrong. You're there to reconcile . . . *in spite of.* You're there because Jesus gave us the ministry of reconciliation. You're there because you are compelled by his love.

God sent his Son into the world not to condone what we're doing but to live in stark contrast in order to let us know that there is a God who loves us.

CHANGING YOUR MIND

For Christ's love compels us, because we are convinced that one died for all, and therefore all died. And he died for all, that those who live should no longer live for themselves but for him who died for them and was raised again.
2 Corinthians 5:14–15

SESSION 5

Our Way, A Way

Raising children is one of life's biggest challenges. It requires all of our strengths and talents. It makes us keenly aware of our weaknesses.

The stakes of parenting are high, yet it requires us to learn on the job. We always feel a step behind. Just when we think we have a child figured out, he or she moves on to a new stage with all new challenges.

To complicate matters, no two children are exactly the same. What we've learned parenting one child doesn't always apply to parenting his or her siblings.

In this session, Andy and Sandra Stanley share some of their experiences as parents. Know this: if you're a single parent, a blended family, or a more non-traditional family, Andy and Sandra claim no

moral authority when it comes to how you should raise your kids—

especially if your family looks different from theirs. Feel free to take

what they say and look at it through the filter of your current reality.

Figure out which parts apply to you and which parts don't.

DISCUSSION STARTER

What were the household rules when you were growing up? How have

those rules influenced your current family life?

WEEKLY READING

Rejection and Acceptance

Psalm 127 says this about children:

> *Children are a heritage from the Lord,*
> *offspring a reward from him.*
> *Like arrows in the hands of a warrior*
> *are children born in one's youth.*
> *Blessed is the man*
> *whose quiver is full of them.*
> *They will not be put to shame*
> *when they contend with their opponents in court.*
> **Psalm 127:3–5**

That's extraordinary. On good days, parents recognize the truth

of those verses. On bad days, raising children feels like a thankless chore. And on the really bad days, parents wonder if they're permanently messing up their kids. Will they end up carrying deep wounds into adulthood that negatively affect their quality of life?

Parenting is complex, but there's one gauge you can keep an eye on in order to maximize your chances of helping your children grow into healthy adults: the amount of acceptance and rejection they experience in their relationship with you.

The massive doses of rejection and acceptance we receive in life shape our souls as human beings. You are who you are because of the acceptance and the rejection you face. This begins at home. To some extent, who you are as an adult is a combination of the mix of rejection and acceptance you received as a child.

It shapes our souls. In some ways, it shapes our personalities. It certainly shapes our responses to events in our lives. Two things in the home affect how much children feel accepted and rejected:

1. The words their parents use

2. The schedules their parents choose

Parents of children and young adolescents tend to obsess over discipline. But it's doubtful you'll look back and regret the way you disciplined your child. Your biggest regrets are more likely to be words you wish you'd said or words you wish had never come out of your mouth. Everything you said may have been true, but you still rejected your children.

Think about it. You've probably forgotten things your parents said that they urged you never to forget. But you remember words that cut you like a knife. They may have been true, but they still hurt. They may have even shaped who you are as an adult.

If you want to avoid making those same mistakes as a parent, decide ahead of time what your children need to hear and then say it ten times more than you think they need to hear it. What is it your daughter needs to hear from her father? What is it your son needs to hear from his mother? What is it your children need to hear? Decide.

The other thing to keep an eye on is the way you handle schedules at home. This is one of the biggest traps parents fall into. We are busy. Our children are busy. But one way we can communicate acceptance to our children is how we spend our time and what we make a priority. We love our children in our hearts, but we have to love them with our calendars and our schedules. Your children can't see what's in your heart, but they can see how you spend your time.

If you prioritize time with your children, they will want to spend time with you when they're older. Parenting is a short season. The days might feel long, but the years are so short. The way we prioritize our time speaks volumes to our kids of acceptance versus rejection.

VIDEO NOTES

_____

_____

_____

_____

_____

_____

_____

_____

_____

_____

_____

_____

_____

_____

_____

_____

_____

_____

DISCUSSION QUESTIONS

1. How are the ways that you discipline your children (or plan to discipline your children) similar to how you were disciplined as a child? How are they different?

2. How did acceptance and rejection during your childhood influence who you are as an adult?

3. If you have children, do you read a family devotion with them? If so, when and how do you read it?

4. What are some things you find most challenging about parenting (or most intimidating about the idea of parenting if you don't yet have children)?

5. Is it easier for you to communicate acceptance to members of your family with your words or with your time and schedule? Why?

6. What can you do now to create the story you want your children to tell about their years growing up? What can this group do to help you?

MOVING FORWARD

If you're currently in the trenches of parenting, your kids will be adults sooner than you think. Every person has a unique story. Each of your children will have a story. You'll be a tremendous part of their stories. No matter what has happened up to this point, now is the time to ask yourself what you can you do now for your children. What can you do to make sure your children have great stories when they're adults?

CHANGING YOUR MIND

Start children off on the way they should go,
and even when they are old they will not turn from it.
Proverbs 22:6

SESSION 6
The Echo

We are who we are because of the people that came before us. We're in the process, whether we give any thought to it or not, of shaping the next generation of our families by what we say and do.

You may have some sense of how your grandparents shaped your parents. You may even have an idea of how your great-grandparents shaped your grandparents. But you probably don't think about how you are somebody's previous generation. Think about that. One day you'll be a snapshot in somebody's mind.

One of the best illustrations of this principle comes from a story in the Old Testament. At the beginning of this study, we said the Old Testament doesn't offer many examples of great families. Instead, most of the families we read about are dysfunctional. This particular story is no different. There's plenty of dysfunction. But it still illustrates the power of generational parenting and thinking in terms of the legacies we leave.

The story takes place over sixty years. In fact, it takes up about two-thirds of the book of Genesis. You're probably familiar with the second half of the story. It's characterized by miracles and epic events. But it only makes full sense within the context provided by the first, less familiar half of the story.

Andy Stanley tells this story in the video that accompanies this session. Kick off your conversation with the Discussion Starter and then watch the video.

DISCUSSION STARTER

Growing up, what stories did you hear about your grandparents or great-grandparents? How did those stories help shape who you are?

WEEKLY READING

They'll Take Their Cue from You

Joseph's story is one of hardship and betrayal. The favoritism of his father made his brothers angry and jealous. They threw him into a pit and then sold him into slavery. Joseph chose to trust God despite his challenging circumstances and rose to become the head servant in the house of his master, Potiphar.

But even that went sour. Falsely accused of wrongdoing by Potiphar's wife, Joseph ended up in prison. There, he met the baker and cupbearer of Pharaoh and correctly interpreted their dreams. Despite his help, the cupbearer forgot about Joseph once he was released from prison. Still, Joseph chose to trust that God was good.

When Pharaoh began having troubling dreams, the cupbearer remembered Joseph. He was summoned from prison to interpret Pharaoh's dreams. Joseph predicted that Egypt would experience seven years of plenty followed by seven years of famine. Pharaoh gave him great authority to plan for and manage the looming crisis. Suddenly, Joseph had gone from prison to the top of Egypt's political system. Joseph remained faithful to God, trusting that he had a plan.

When the famine finally came, it drove Joseph's brothers to Egypt in search of food. There, they came face to face with the brother they'd betrayed. When they realized it was Joseph who managed Egypt's storehouse of food, they were terrified. This was their brother's chance for revenge. He had all the power . . . and all the food.

But Joseph, instead of paying his brothers back, gathered them together and said something extraordinary to them:

But Joseph said to them, "Don't be afraid. Am I in the place of God? You intended to harm me, but God intended it for good to accomplish what is now being done, the saving of many lives. So then, don't be afraid. I will provide for you and your children." And he reassured them and spoke kindly to them.
Genesis 50:19–21

It's not just that Joseph was forgiving. It's that he trusted God with the outcomes of his circumstances—good and bad. Joseph didn't respond that way simply because that's how he was wired. He responded that way because earlier generations of his family had wrestled with their circumstances and God was always in the center of the action. Joseph had grown up hearing stories about his grandparents and great-grandparents that demonstrated God's faithfulness.

The echo of previous generations taught Joseph that God could be trusted.

The moral of the story of Joseph and his family is that what your children, grandchildren, nieces, and nephews see you do will lay the groundwork for what they will do in times of crisis. They'll forget almost everything you say. They won't forget who you are. They won't forget what you did when things were going well and when they were going poorly.

The examples they'll take away will be from what you do when staying is difficult; when not paying your debts would be easier; when mishandling your money would be more fun. They won't remember your words, but they will remember your actions.

If you're a dad, you're a role model for how the next generations will treat their wives and daughters. If you're a mom, you're a role model for how they will treat their husbands and sons. If you're a parent, you're the role model for how your children will raise your grandchildren. You're the role model for how they should deal with extraordinary temptation. You're the role model for how they should respond to crises. Odds are, future generations will take their cue from you.

VIDEO NOTES

_____

_____

_____

_____

_____

_____

_____

_____

_____

_____

_____

_____

_____

_____

_____

_____

_____

_____

_____

DISCUSSION QUESTIONS

1. Do you agree with the idea that when it comes to raising children, what you do has more weight than what you say? Why or why not?

2. Talk about a time when you saw a parent or grandparent wrestling with difficult circumstances. How did that person's response to those circumstances—good or bad—influence you?

3. How do you usually respond under pressure? Why?

4. What are three words you want to describe the characteristics of your children and grandchildren?

5. What would you do differently if you knew that your children will eventually take their cues from what you do rather than what you say?

6. What is one thing you can do this week to begin to change how your life will echo in the lives of your children, grandchildren, and great-grandchildren? What can this group do to support you?

MOVING FORWARD

Actions don't just speak louder than words, sometimes they echo into the next generation. Your actions aren't just about here and now. They aren't just about the next ten or fifteen years. Some of your actions will echo into the next generation of your future family.

By God's grace maybe one day you'll be a grandparent. Maybe you'll be a great-grandparent. What will echo from your life into those future generations? You have a greater opportunity than perhaps you ever imagined. You can respond to temptation now; manage your money now; respond to relational crises now in such a way that it reverberates into your future family.

If this is true, what should you do differently? If this is true then what do you need to change? If this is true why wouldn't you change as soon as possible?

CHANGING YOUR MIND

In everything set them an example by doing what is good. In your teaching show integrity..."
Titus 2:7

F·U·T·U·R·E FAMILY

LEADER'S GUIDE

LEADER'S GUIDE

This Leader's Guide contains helpful tips for using these *Future Family* materials with your group.

USING THE FUTURE FAMILY
PARTICIPANT'S GUIDE

Before Each Group Meeting

1. Read the "Introduction" and "Weekly Reading" sections in this guide.

2. Watch the video segment for the session on the DVD.

3. Answer the "Discussion Questions."

4. Review the "Moving Forward" section.

5. Send your group members an email.

   - Introduce the meeting's topic.

   - Ask them to read the session materials and answer the "Discussion Questions."

   - Confirm the date, time, and location of your next meeting.

During Each Group Meeting

1. Read the "Introduction" in this guide aloud.

2. Use the "Discussion Starter" to help your group ease in to the conversation.

3. Read the "Weekly Reading" in this guide aloud.

4. Watch the video segment on the DVD.

5. Have a conversation based on your answers to the "Discussion Questions."

6. Read the "Moving Forward" section aloud.

SETTING EXPECTATIONS

Different group members will have different ideas about what happens during group meetings, so it's important to set expectations. Some will want more social time. Others will want "serious" study. Still others will be contemplative types who want to spend a lot of time praying.

Social time, study, and prayer are all important to a great group experience. You can decide as a group how much time you want to spend in each. The important thing is that everyone knows what to expect.

A typical group meeting might be structured as follows:

- **30 minutes**—Social time (you can serve coffee and dessert during this time; some groups even share a meal together)
- **1 hour**—Bible, book, video, or curriculum study (it's a good idea to begin this portion of the evening with a short prayer)
- **30 minutes**—Prayer requests and prayer

FACILITATING THE DISCUSSION

Here are five things to consider while facilitating the discussion during your group meetings:

CULTIVATE DISCUSSION

It's easy to assume that a group meeting succeeds or fails based on the quality of your ideas. That's not true. It's the ideas of everyone in the group that make a small group meeting successful. Your role is to create an environment in which people feel safe to share their thoughts.

POINT TO THE MATERIAL

Sometimes you'll simply read a discussion question and invite everyone to respond. The conversation will take care of itself. At other times, you may need to encourage group members to share their ideas. Go with the flow, but be ready to nudge the conversation in the right direction when necessary.

DEPART FROM THE MATERIAL

You don't have to stick rigidly to the Discussion Questions in this guide. Knowing when to depart from them is more art than science, but no one knows more about your group than you do.

STAY ON TRACK

This is the flip side to the previous point. While you want to leave space for group members to think through the discussion, make sure the conversation is contributing to the bottom line for the week. Don't let it veer off on tangents. Politely refocus the group.

PRAY

This is the most important thing you can do as a leader. Pray for your group members. Pray for your own leadership. Pray that God is not only present at your group meetings, but is directing them.